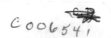
DATE DUE			

Written by **Karen Romano Young**
Illustrated by **Doug Cushman**

ideals®

Nelson Place at Elm Hill Pike
Nashville, Tennessee 37214

Titles in the Best Behavior™ Series

PLEASE COME TO MY PARTY...

EXCUSE ME, MAY I HAVE AN EXTRA NAPKIN?

PLEASE, MAY I HAVE A PENCIL?

EXCUSE ME, YOU'RE STANDING IN

    FRONT OF THE TV...

PARDON ME, IS THIS SEAT TAKEN?

EXCUSE ME, BUT IT'S MY TURN . . .

Published by Ideals Publishing Corporation

Produced for Ideals Publishing Corporation by
Joshua Morris Publishing, Inc.
167 Old Post Road, Southport, Connecticut 06490

Printed in Singapore

Home! It's your own special place.

At home, you don't need to think about manners — or do you?

You spend more time at home than anywhere else. You also spend more time with your family than with anyone else. They're built-in friends to talk with . . .

eat with. . .

play with. . .

relax with. . .

You may share your home with other people including. . .

parents and grandparents. . .

brothers and sisters, cousins, aunts or uncles. . .

and visitors. . .

Afterall, it's people that make a home special. The mood of your home may be sour or sweet. Often it depends on how *you* act. As often as you can. . .

be fair. . .

be understanding and thoughtful. Help with chores. If you know something needs doing, pitch in and help get a job done.

Everyone has different needs and feelings. It's important to. . .

not snoop. . .

not eavesdrop. . .

not be a blabbermouth. . .

When you share a room, try to cooperate. Divide things fairly.

Don't mess around with someone's work or belongings.

If you share the telephone, always be polite. Don't say funny things when you answer the phone.

You never know who might be calling. Your rudeness could cost a family member a friend, date or job!

Don't give too many reasons why someone can't come to the phone.

Don't hog the phone. If someone is expecting an important call, stay off the phone.

Take complete messages, and be sure someone knows that they have a message left for them. Leave the message where it is sure to be noticed.

When you share the TV, try to be fair. If you want to watch something special, let everyone know ahead of time. Take turns watching regular programs.

In general. . .

Be neat. When you share any room with others — especially the kitchen and bathroom — don't be piggy. Don't leave a mess for someone else to clean up!

If you borrow something, bring it back in the same condition that you found it.

Most families take turns sharing household chores. If it's your turn to help with the dishes or carry out the garbage, do it cheerfully. Don't argue! If you don't feel well, or have another activity planned, politely ask another family member to take your turn.

If you share a pet, do what's best for the pet. Divide the fun as well as the chores.

Be respectful. Don't talk back or argue. Instead talk things over calmly.

If someone is sick, or angry or upset, be nice about it. Try to think of ways to make things easier.

You can't get along with everyone all the time. If you have an argument, take time to cool down and think. Try to solve the problem calmly. If you need to, ask someone to help with the problem.

Sometimes, families don't all live in one household. If you go to stay with a parent or any relative, follow their house rules.

Don't compare one home to another.

Don't spy on one parent for the other.

There may be times when a babysitter will have to stay with you. Try to be friendly and polite.

Remember, this person is not familiar with the household. Help them as much as you can.

If someone has good news let *them* tell it. Everyone has a touchy spot so don't tease!

Don't tell on someone unless it's an emergency.

Remember. . .

Be as polite to your family as you would to anyone else. Say "Excuse me," not "get out of my way!"

Don't tag along unless you're invited.

In public, always be supportive of your family.

Your home is special.
Your family is special.
How well it works, is often up to you!